"In diversity there is beauty and there
is strength." Maya Angelou (2014)

The Kids' Book of
DIVERSITY

Catherine Stephenson. Illustrated by Hiruni Kariyawasam

There's a new boy in Daniela and Dustin's class, called Shaluka. Shaluka is from Sri Lanka.

Daniela and Dustin wonder what Sri Lanka is like. Do they speak a different language? Are the children different there? They look around their class. Why do people have different color skin?

Do you know?

Follow Daniela and Dustin on a journey to find out the ways in which people are different, and the ways in which they are the same.

Our homes are DIFFERENT.

Children might live in a city, in the countryside, in a desert, in the mountains, on an island or by the sea. Everywhere on earth, there are children.

Children live in houses, apartments, tents, houseboats, caravans or any other type of home.

Daniela and Dustin live
in an apartment block.

Shaluka lives in a house.

What is your home like?

Our families are DIFFERENT.

Daniela and Dustin live with their mum and their grandma.

Some children live with two parents, some live with one, some live with a grandparent, with a foster family or with another carer.

You might be the only child living at home, or there might be lots of children.

There are many types of family, but they are all great if the members love and care for each other and keep each other safe.

When you grow up, you can choose the person or people you love and have a family of your own.

We speak DIFFERENTLY.

Dustin and Daniela have a different accent than Shaluka.
Shaluka can speak a completely different language too.

Some people can even talk with their hands
using sign language to communicate.

There could be someone near you who speaks a different
language. They might have come from another country — or
their family came from another country many years ago.

Can you think of anyone?

Celebrating differences is what the world should do, And sharing similarities is quite essential.

රූප කථා පොත සැකසූ
කතුවරයාගේ අදහස් වැදගත්ය
මෙම රූප කථා පොත

Es porque somos diferentes que cada uno de nosotros es especial. Together we can do so much. Alone we can do so little.

Unes mans petites poden canviar el mon

We have DIFFERENT customs and traditions.

People around the world have different ways of doing things: we have different religions, eat different foods, might dress differently, or sing different songs.

We even have different parties.

What special days does your family celebrate?

We are DIFFERENT colors.

Skin keeps our insides in, and germs and bacteria out!

Skin and hair comes in many different shades and textures. Even people in your family might have different ones.

Daniela and Dustin have warm beige skin, amber eyes and dark brown hair. Shaluka has deep brown skin and brown eyes.

What are your eyes, skin and hair like?

Our bodies work DIFFERENTLY.

Dustin wears glasses. He has a big smile from ear to ear.

George talks using sign language. He also uses pictures to request his favourite toys.

Clara is a wheelchair user. She loves playing for her basketball team.

If you see a child that looks different from you, you could try asking them their name and telling them yours.

We are DIFFERENT sizes and DIFFERENT shapes.

People can be short, tall, big, small, extra big or extra small. We come in all sorts of sizes, and all sorts of shapes!

The human body is truly amazing. Think how you grow, the things you learn to do and the places your body can take you.

Your unique body, together with all
the stuff inside — how you feel, what
you think and the things you like —
are what makes you YOU.

We have DIFFERENT strengths.

People can have many different qualities. Our differences make us strong when we work together!

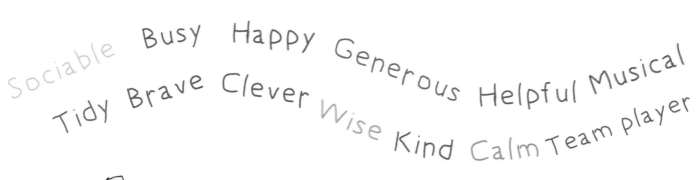

Sociable Busy Happy Generous Helpful Musical Tidy Brave Clever Wise Kind Calm Team player

Daniela enjoys drawing and solving puzzles. She needs some help with learning to read.

Creative Curious Funny

Loving Adventurous Giving

Dustin is thoughtful and good at
caring for others. He sometimes needs
encouragement to try new things.

What do you find easy and
what do you find more difficult?

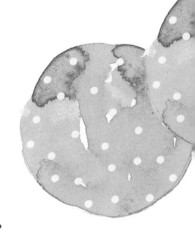

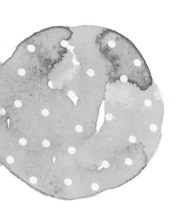

We have DIFFERENT feelings.

Daniela loves surprises, whereas Dustin likes
to know what is going to happen in advance.

Dustin finds it hard to wait
whereas Daniela is very relaxed.

Daniela loves cuddles but Dustin
likes to have his own space.

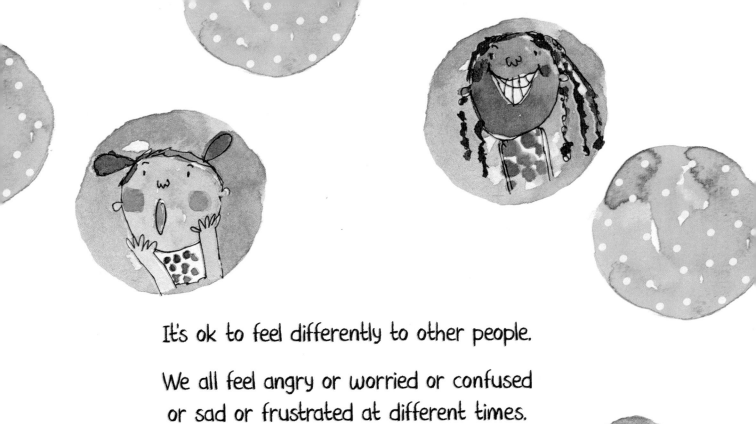

It's ok to feel differently to other people.

We all feel angry or worried or confused
or sad or frustrated at different times.
Different things make us feel different ways.

Who could you talk to if you're
worried about something?

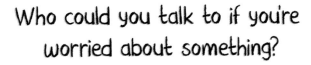

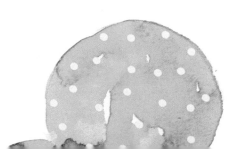

Be DIFFERENT. Be YOU!

There are lots of ways to show the
world who you are: how you dress,
your hairstyle, the colours you like
and the things you enjoy doing.

Dustin loves animals and nature, doing
magic tricks and baking cakes for his family.

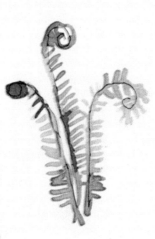

Daniela loves singing, drawing, bright colors and climbing.

Don't be afraid to do your own thing. Sometimes you will be different from the people around you. That's ok. There will be others who like the things that you like too.

We can learn to respect DIFFERENCES.

You won't always agree with or understand what someone else thinks or how they behave. But try to be open to different ideas and ways of being.

You don't have to think the same as someone else to live alongside each other peacefully.

Be a champion for DIFFERENCES.

Everyone has the right to be treated fairly and spoken to with kind words. And nobody should ever be excluded or made fun of.

You could try playing with or chatting to someone who is different to you in some way.

And if you hear someone being unkind about someone else's differences, stand up to them if it feels safe, or otherwise speak to a trusted adult.

Different is FUN!

Everyone's different, but we are all human!
You never know who might make a great
friend – someone to play with, laugh with
and share with.

Connecting with different people is one
of the very best things in life.

There's a whole world of
differences out there to discover.
What are you waiting for? :)

let's celebrate you being you! What makes you unique?

My name is ....

I like wearing...

My favorite food is...

Something I love about my body is..

I sometimes get upset when...

I am learning how to....

I sometimes find these things tricky...

My favorite color is...

My favorite toy or game is...

I feel happy when...

Some of the awesome things I can do are...

Some of my special people are...

I like to play...

While other children may have some similar answers, your combined answers make you unique and special.

Now think about a friend (or family member).

My friend's name is ....

- Think of something that is special about your friend.

....

- In what ways are you and your friend similar?

....

- In what ways are you and your friend different?

....

- What would it be like if we all liked the same things?

....

- Why is it good we are all different?

....

Find someone who...

Now it's time to be a detective. Who do you know that...

Has a pet	Is a creative person
Can speak another language	Has a different kind of family to you
Likes to make people laugh	Plays a sport

Was born in a different country to you	Goes to a place of worship
Has parents that were born in a different country	Likes to read
Is good with numbers	Has a different eye color to you

Things I like about me.

Think of as many things as you can that you like about yourself.

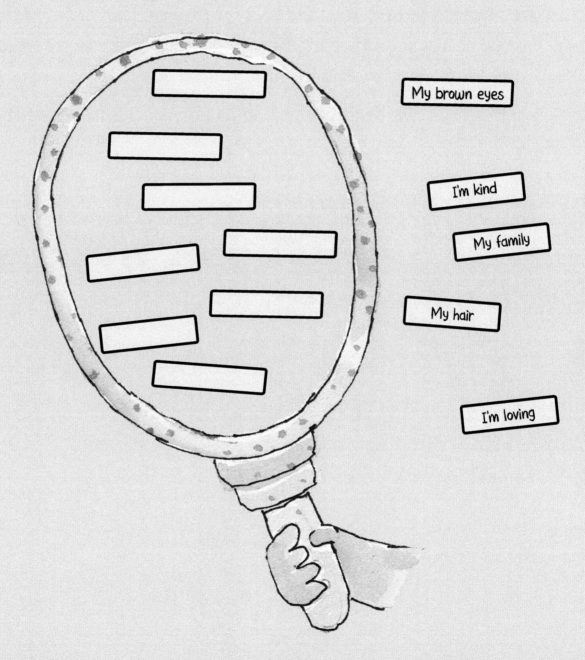

My brown eyes

I'm kind

My family

My hair

I'm loving

Dear Reader,

Thank you for choosing to read *The Kids' Book of Diversity* with your child – I hope you enjoyed it. If you could spare a few minutes to leave me a review on Amazon, I'd love to recieve your feedback.

This book forms part of The Kids' Books of Social Emotional Learning series, which also includes:

Thank you so much for your support and interest in our books!

Catherine
woodenhousebooks.com

To Espai Aigua, our "different" and wonderful primary school in Barcelona.

And to Hiruni, for her gorgeous artwork and for sharing a little piece of Sri Lanka. Hi Shaluka!

First Printing, 2023
Wooden House Books
www.woodenhousebooks.com

About the author and the illustrator.

Catherine (author)

Catherine was born in the UK and grew up in Wales. She now lives with her partner, son and two cats in Barcelona. She is a freelance writer and translator from Spanish and Catalan into English. Her other books include *The Kids' Book of Friends* and the dual language book *Alice and the White Rabbit*. Away from work, you'll find her in the mountains with a camera round her neck, or in the middle of an epic board game with her family.

Hiruni (illustrator)

Hiruni is from Sri Lanka, where she lives with her family in a town called Ambalangoda. She holds a Bachelor's Degree in Fashion Design from the Univversity of Moratuwa. She enjoys doing paintings, fine illustrations, and especially illustrations for children's books in her unique style, mixing digital and watercolour techniques. In her free time, she's also an avid reader.

You can find us at:

WOODEN HOUSE BOOKS

woodenhousebooks.com
IG @woodenhousebooks

Made in the USA
Las Vegas, NV
10 October 2023